PIAZZA

Italy's Heart & Soul

THE UMBRIAN HILLTOWN OF GUBBIO
holds an annual crossbow competition with the
neighboring town of Sansepolcro. Before the actual competition
Gubbio's renowned sbandieratori (flag wavers) perform for admiring crowds
in the town's main square, Piazza Grande. The competition began in
the 12th century and the performers still dress in period costumes.
The colorful silk flags are hand-painted by local artists.

— Foreword —

IF I AM REMEMBERED FOR ANYTHING IN MY PROFESSIONAL LIFE, it will be my photographic work in the Vatican and close ties with Pope John Paul II. For years, it had been my dream to cover ~~that in the world's smallest nation~~, the seat of the Roman Catholic

its moods, ever-changing light, and human activity are the dimensions that every artist hopes for.

Joe and Marybeth also had a dream… to follow their love for Italy and capture the heart and soul of the *piazza*. This book, *Piazza: Italy's Heart & Soul*, has evolved as friendships do, with interest, followed by familiarity and respect.

It is most gratifying to witness your students enthusiastically carrying on where their teachers have left off. As photojournalists, their skill lies in their ability to enter into the flow of peoples' lives. To arrive on the scene a complete stranger in a foreign land and insert yourself into someone's private life demands tact, confidence, and patience. Camera techniques are only a small part of the equation. Henry David Thoreau once wrote, "The question is not what you look at, but what you see."

Our authors have managed to reach out and touch the subject, illustrating how the *piazza* plays a significant role in every aspect of an Italian's life, from intensely personal moments to shared public events. They have succeeded at making us emotionally feel exactly what they felt while capturing the moment. We feel as though we've been there, as you will discover within the pages of this marvelous book.

— *James L. Stanfield*
NATIONAL GEOGRAPHIC PHOTOGRAPHER

ELITE CARABINIERI GUARDS perform in St. Peter's Square on April 19, 2005, at the election of Pope Benedict XVI. Amidst all the pomp and ceremony the huge, enthusiastic crowd that gathered in the piazza buzzed with excitement.

EVERY YEAR ON MAY 15th
the town of Gubbio celebrates the
Ceri Marathon, an event packed
with emotion. A massive crowd
gathers in Gubbio's Piazza
Grande to watch the raising of
the ceri, heavy wooden structures

ceri from the piazza to the top of
the mountain above Gubbio.

Following pages:

AN ANCIENT FOOTPATH
along the shores of the Ligurian
Sea connects the five towns of
the Cinque Terre and provides a
bird's-eye view of the seaside
piazza in Vernazza. A medieval
fortress and castle that was
once used as a lookout for
pirates is perched on the rocks
above town.

A PHOTOGRAPHIC TOUR
through Italy's town squares
reveals that everyone loves the
piazza, especially children.

7

DURING A QUIET MOMENT, the lights along Venice's Grand Canal illuminate the surface of the calm water. The domes of the majestic baroque church, Santa Maria della Salute, loom above the palazzos along the waterfront. The church was built in the 17th century and is dedicated to the Virgin Mary in gratitude for ending the plague of 1630-1631, which killed 47,000 Venetians.

AN ANTIQUE BOAT
floats regally in a procession during Venice's historical regatta, which is held on the first Sunday of September. Boatmen dress in medieval costumes and thousands of spectators line both sides of the Grand Canal. A series of boat races follows in which competitors test their formidable rowing skills against one another.

PIAZZA

Italy's Heart & Soul

TEXT AND PHOTOGRAPHY BY

JOE BAUWENS

MARYBETH FLOWER

Eccola
PRESS

*with several Romanesque elements. During the 11ᵗʰ century
the city rulers planned to make the Duomo the largest church in
Christendom but the Black Plague intervened, tragically
decimating the population of Siena.*

TEXT & PHOTOGRAPHY:
Joe Bauwens & Marybeth Flower

ART DIRECTOR & DESIGN EDITOR:
Constance Hoffman Phelps

EDITOR:
Carrie J. Lightner

PRE-PRESS:
TRI-DIGITAL GROUP
Ray Reed & Jim Armstrong

PRINTING:
Worzalla

PUBLISHER'S CATALOGING-IN-PUBLICATION

Bauwens, Joe.
   Piazza : Italy's heart and soul / text, Joe Bauwens &
Marybeth Flower ; photography, Joe Bauwens & Marybeth
Flower.
   p. cm.
   LCCN 2006929890
   ISBN 0-9787424-7-8

   1. Plazas--Italy--Pictorial works. 2. Architecture
and society--Italy--Pictorial works. 3. Italy--Social
life and customs--Pictorial works. 4. Italy--
Description and travel--Pictorial works.   I. Flower,
Marybeth. II. Title.

NA9070.B38 2006   711'.55'0945
                                   QBI06-600335

Printed and bound in the United States.

HORSES RACE AROUND THE PIAZZA
during Siena's Palio, the most famous festival in Italy.
Three horses lean into the treacherous second turn.
During the race two riders fell at this spot and were
rushed to the hospital. Luckily they were released
with only minor injuries just a few hours later.

18

CONTENTS

ITALY

This book includes photographs from piazze throughout Italy. The map of Italy (left) shows the location of towns and cities where the 25 piazze presented in this book are situated. These towns range from areas near the borders of France, Switzerland, Austria, and Slovenia to the island of Sicily,

Cortina d'Ampezzo

FRIULI-
VENEZIA
GIULIA
• Udine

TRENTINO-ALTO-ADIGE

• Aosta
VALLE D'AOSTA

• Orta
San Giulio

LOMBARDY

VENETO

• Verona   • Padua

Venice

GULF OF

SEA

TUSCANY   • Arezzo

• Siena

• Gubbio

Val d'Orcia •

UMBRIA

MARCHES

• Norcia

Orvieto •

ADRIATIC SEA

ABRUZZI

Sutri •

LATIUM

VATICAN CITY ★

Rome •

ITALY

MOLISE

GULF OF
GAETA

CAMPANIA

APULIA

• Locorotondo

SARDINIA

BASILICATA

TYRRHENIAN SEA

CALABRIA

GULF OF
TARANTO

IONIAN
SEA

Cefalù •

N

• Taormina

SICILY

MEDITERRANEAN SEA

0 miles   50   100

Oliver Uberti

21

Cappuccino is a drink invented in Italy and favored by Italians in the mornings.

The *piazza* is the heart and soul of an Italian town. It is where Italy truly comes alive. The town square never sleeps; it is filled with the sounds and smells of Italian life at almost every hour of the day. Yet it is so much more than just a neighborhood park—it is a living, breathing entity with a distinct personality. A day in the *piazza* overflows with music, romance, laughter, aromas of fresh *espresso* or tomato sauce cooking, and the richness of Italian culture.

Entering a *piazza* can be like stepping back in time; beautiful historic churches share the square with bustling cafés and shops. The *piazza* often occupies the most picturesque spot in town. There is something special about the light in an Italian *piazza*—it can have an almost dreamlike quality and glows with a warmth and vitality that is unique to Italy.

Town squares have played a significant role in Italy's history and culture for more than 2,000 years. During the time of the Roman Empire a *piazza* was called a forum. Citizens and officials used them mainly for open-air markets and political speeches. Brutal public executions took place in town squares in the Middle Ages. Throughout the entire span of Italy's rich and varied history, a *piazza* has been a place to gather. All of its different functions and uses have evolved and coalesced into the *piazza* as it is today.

People of all ages come to the local square to see and be seen. They congregate there to hear the latest gossip and to spend time with family and friends. For an Italian, it would be hard to say which is more important—a kitchen with a big communal table or the local *piazza*. The concept is so important to Italians that they redesigned the medals for the 2006 Winter Olympics in Torino to include a hole in the middle symbolizing the *piazza*, the center of Italian life.

For most Italians, life in the *piazza* starts at an early age. Children first come in strollers or baby carriages. Some mothers breastfeed their newborn babies in the *piazza*. Men and women of all ages coo over the *bambini*, as children are called in Italy. As soon as they can toddle, kids start chasing pigeons in the square and learn to play with soccer balls.

Italy's children use the *piazza* as a personal playground. Many boys and girls practice riding a first

the entire community.

A friend of ours, who lives outside of Lucca, brings his daughter to the local town square every Saturday morning. She plays with other children her age while he and his wife mingle with friends. Young boys and girls eagerly look forward to weekend outings to the *piazza* where friendships form and flourish. It is the cornerstone of social life in Italy. Roberto, another acquaintance from Lucca, told us that when he was young, before every family had a telephone, the *piazza* was where all communication took place. He recalled Saturday evening teen dances when it was essential to bring a date. Every Thursday night he went to the square with the eager hope of finding a girl to take to Saturday's dance.

The *piazza* is an important place throughout the entire life span of an Italian. Baptisms, First Communions, confirmations, weddings, and funerals all take place in the church on the square. On occasion, religious ceremonies spill out into the *piazza* and priests and nuns are a common sight among the regulars. Sometimes Italian funeral processions parade through the square with a brass band. Children grow up spending a lot of time in the *piazza* and then bring their own families to the square later in life. Many people have found love and met spouses there. It is not uncommon to see young lovers strolling through a *piazza*, holding hands or locked in a passionate embrace.

In addition to being the social center of town, the *piazza* is also a bustling marketplace for fruits, vegetables, cheeses, meats, and an endless array of other goods. Non-motorized pedestrian streets with charming shops often lead into the *piazza* and life tends to spill out into them. Of course, there is always at least one *gelato* shop in or near the central square. In the late afternoon and evening the markets are usually replaced with outdoor cafés, bars, and restaurants that bring people together to talk, mingle, and watch other people.

On many occasions, modern-day street performers entertain people in the *piazza* across a wide spectrum of the arts. Mimes, people mimicking statues, acrobats, singers, and musicians playing a myriad of instruments all compete for attention. The *piazza* is the town's central stage or outdoor theater for reenacting centuries-old pageants such as horse races, football games, jousts, medieval parades, and crossbow competitions, as well as for celebrating numerous patron saints' feast days.

A lively feature of events in the *piazza* is often a performance by colorfully dressed *sbandieratori*—flag twirlers and throwers dressed in medieval garb. Boys in Italy begin learning this art when they are only eight or nine years old and continue training throughout early adulthood. The young boys work with one flag and as they become more adept, they advance to handling five or six flags simultaneously. Master *sbandieratori* are sometimes introduced by name to the warm applause of a passionately adoring crowd. Spectators go wild over the thrilling *sbandieratori* performances which are a part of most medieval festivals.

Piazze are also hubs of political activity. Throngs of people fill a town's square during rallies for political parties or causes. Sometimes important referendum committees organize huge concerts in *piazze* in large cities. The media occasionally uses the square as a background for interviews with local politicians.

When the *piazza* is not teeming with people during special events and celebrations, life follows certain rhythmical patterns. On weekdays many older people typically mill around the square, but there always seem to be more men than women. Many retired men spend time in the *piazza* watching people, engaging in animated conversations with friends, or playing cards. The men often stand or sit in groups. During the winter they follow the sun around the square and in the summer months they chase the shade.

The "silent dinner bell" is another phenomenon that occurs in *piazze* throughout all of Italy. The square is usually abuzz with activity between six and eight o'clock in the evening. At eight o'clock it empties as though a silent bell has rung and everyone goes home for the evening meal. In the summer after dinner the *piazza* begins to fill up again and young children play in the square until nearly midnight. During the day it is typically empty from one o'clock to three-thirty in the afternoon and all the surrounding shops are closed for the midday break.

Sunday mornings are a special time in the *piazza*. Churchgoers like to stop at the local café to enjoy a *cappuccino* or an *espresso*. Men and women sit, surrounded by a sea of newspapers, completely engrossed. Some café regulars perch at tables for hours with stacks of papers. On Sundays it is common to see multi-generational families spending time together in the *piazza*.

Cafés in the *piazza* are very important meeting spots. Often there is more than one café in the square. Most people, who live nearby, stop for a morning coffee on the way to work. The cafés are typically buzzing with activity, whether it is workers taking a break or people gathering after a long day to meet friends, swap stories, or play a lively card game.

The Italian custom of *passeggiata*, when townspeople stroll through the *piazza* dressed in their finery, meeting and greeting friends, is especially delightful. Saturday and Sunday evenings are the most popular times for this tradition. The *piazza* comes alive and throbs with activity. People of all ages fill the square, gesturing wildly and carrying on animated discussions. It is during times like this that the vibrancy and passion of the Italian *piazza* is most palpable.

Piazze come in all styles, shapes, and sizes. The square in Orto San Giulio sits next to a beautiful lake, Gubbio's *piazza* is medieval and clings to the side of a steep hill, and Vatican City's Piazza San Pietro is majestic and baroque in style. Many include a central feature such as a fountain or a statue where people gather. There are places in all *piazze* for people to sit, whether at the base of a fountain, on the steps of a church, or on stone benches situated around the perimeter. Often the local Catholic church,

Venice, Piazza della Signoria in Florence, Piazza del Campo in Siena, and Piazza San Pietro in the Vatican. In addition, we have featured a number of small towns with magical *piazze* such as Piazza Grande in Gubbio, Piazza San Benedetto in Norcia (remotely situated in mountainous eastern Umbria), and Piazza del Comune in Sutri, just outside of Rome.

We first toyed with the idea for this book during one of our many trips to Italy. On that particular trip we visited a different hill town every day. We spent most of the day in the town's *piazza*, simply watching life unfold and noticing that in spite of many similarities, each square had its own distinct rhythm and personality. We thought that someone should put together a photographic book about life in the Italian *piazza*. Years later, we mentioned the idea to a

A wedding couple toasts with friends in Cortona's Piazza della Repubblica.

friend who is a professional photographer. She was enthusiastic but could not devote enough time to taking all the images herself. She suggested we do the book on our own.

It became apparent to us that in order to truly capture the soul of the *piazza*, we needed to spend a significant amount of time in each one. We invested a year in intensive photography workshops and embarked on a five-month trip to Italy. By crisscrossing the country many times to document celebrations, festivals, patron saints' days, weddings, baptisms, first communions, and funerals, we learned about everyday life in the *piazza*. These photographs pay tribute to all the *piazze* in Italy and to the essential role they play in the country's past, present, and future. It has been an incredible journey for us and has deepened our love affair with Italy, its people, customs, and language.

Venice

Mysterious, alluring, captivating, and sensual, Venice is often referred to as the "Queen of the Adriatic." It is a place of wonder where light and clouds reflect on the dazzling water and create a magical ambiance that changes with every moment. As the sun's rays mingle with foggy mist, the city glistens through a shimmering veil.

Venice is built upon a series of tiny islands interconnected by canals and pedestrian bridges. Waterways serve as thoroughfares, making Venice the most unique city in the world. With no roads or cars, everything moves by boat, including the fire department. Even the noisy motor scooters, ubiquitous in Italy, are absent.

The city was settled when mainlanders fled from invading barbarians. The Republic of Venice came into existence in 697 with the election of the first *doge* and continued for more than 1,000 years, making it the world's longest lasting republic. Because of its longevity it was called La Serenissima, or "the most serene republic."

Piazza San Marco, the heart of Venice, is one of the most beautiful squares known to man. It has been called the "drawing room of the world." During the days of La Serenissima, it was the religious and political center of the city. In addition to serving as a gathering place, the square was designed to flaunt the republic's prosperity. The Basilica of San Marco (right) gleams in the sunlight and the Doge's Palace instills a sense of power and wealth. The *piazza* is a very festive place. Students dressed in elegant 17th century costumes and wigs stroll around selling concert tickets. The cafés in the square compete with one another for patrons to listen to lively classical music (above) that fills the *piazza* with wonderful sounds.

VENICE IS BUILT on 117 small islands. The busiest place in the city is San Marco Square. Throngs of people are drawn to it because of the elaborate basilica with magnificent

well-dressed waiter at Café Florian (right) brings refreshments to his customers. Florian's is a Venetian institution and Europe's oldest coffee house.

29

GONDOLE AND ELABORATE MASKS are synonymous with Venice. In this city creating them is considered an art. A carnival reveler pauses in Piazza San Marco (above). Gliding through the narrow canals of Venice in a handcrafted gondola (left) is a delight to the senses. For centuries, gondole served as the city's main mode of transportation. In recent years adding elaborate decoration to the vessels has become very popular; however, there is a movement underway to eliminate gold leaf trimmings and brightly colored cushions in order to be more historically accurate.

THE CUPOLAS OF SANTA MARIA DELLA SALUTE and the smokestacks of a cruise ship tower over the Grand Canal, Venice's main thoroughfare (below). Regata Storico participants parade through Campo Santo Stefano sumptuously dressed in period costumes (following pages). Venice has staged this historical regatta since the late 13th century.

BURANO, AN ISLAND in the northern portion of the Venetian Lagoon, is a colorful fishing village.
All of its houses and buildings are painted in brilliant colors. Burano is also famous
for its exquisite handmade lace. In recent years, ever since the lace-making school on the island
closed, most of it is imported from China.

WALKING THROUGH BURANO *is like walking through a rainbow. Even on a gloomy day the town's colors sizzle. Perhaps it is a reflection of Burano's well-known fierce independence. Children walk past Casa Deo "Bepi Suà," a colorful house painted with geometric designs located in a tiny square on the island.*

AT THE HEIGHT OF THE 17TH CENTURY *there were thousands of gondole floating in Venice's canals. Today the number has dwindled to approximately 500 and they are used primarily by tourists. A gondolier (above) gazes out at Canale di San Marco and the church of San Giorgio as moored gondole (right) bob in the water at the edge of Piazza San Marco.*

38

Padua

Padua is first and foremost a university town. It is home to the famous University of Padua, one of the oldest and most prestigious in Europe. It was originally named the University of Bo; Galileo Galilei was a professor there from 1592 to 1610. In contrast to the tradition in the United States of holding a mass graduation ceremony in the early summer, students in Padua graduate in small groups throughout the year as they pass their final tests. It is a long-held tradition for family and friends to taunt graduates as they walk through the central *piazze* by singing a raunchy song that begins, "*Dottore! Dottore! Dottore!*" The friendly taunting often includes large, off-color caricatures of the graduates that are hung along the main pedestrian street for all passersby to see. The excited students wear laurel wreaths on their heads and costumes that range from conservative to downright bawdy.

During the day, Padua's two main *piazze*, Piazza della Frutta and Piazza delle Erbe, come alive with markets and gourmet specialty shops (below). In the evenings the bars and cafés take over the scene as they fill up with boisterous university students and colorful local characters.

Piazza delle Erbe (right) is reflected in the windshield of this bus, "Diretto Piazze," which services the squares.

PADUA IS A BUSY UNIVERSITY TOWN. Students are everywhere in the city core. Graduates proudly don laurel wreaths on graduation day and celebrate

with family and friends. In the late afternoon students swarm the outdoor cafés in the piazze. Cafés replace the market stalls that fill the squares during the morning hours.

Verona

Verona's lively Piazza Bra never seems to sleep. Day and night the plentiful cafés and restaurants overflow with people. It is one of the biggest *piazze* in all of Italy. A park with a small fountain sits in the center of the square and children love to play there under the watchful eyes of parents and grandparents.

During the summer months Verona is an opera lover's paradise. Puccini's "Turandot" (right) is performed in a gigantic Roman arena that is nearly two millenia old. The arena, set within Piazza Bra, is world renowned for its opera staging and draws fans from all over Europe and the United States. In addition to opera, Verona is the home of Shakespeare's Juliet and entices many tourists to its banks along the Adige River.

Via Mazzini, a thriving pedestrian street lined with chic shops, links Piazza Bra to Piazza delle Erbe. Originally a forum during Roman times, Piazza delle Erbe is now lined with hip outdoor cafés. A small outdoor market is held in the *piazza* every day selling souvenirs, fruits, and vegetables.

A large sign advertises a performance of "Carmen" with the Roman Arena in the background (above).

IN THE SUMMER, opera takes over a section of the piazza to store the sets. Stagehands move "Aida" sets from the square into the arena in time for an evening performance (left). A stunningly costumed performer in "Turandot" delights the audience (right).

46

VIA MAZZINI, with its many colorful boutiques, is a feast for the eyes. Stylish shoppers are always strolling and admiring beautiful items in the windows.

*PEOPLE-WATCHING IN PIAZZA BRA is always exciting. A group of elegantly dressed opera-goers
approaches one of the many outdoor restaurants in the square (above). Street performers in Piazza Bra are
ubiquitous. A mime performs for a mesmerized crowd in the piazza (right).*

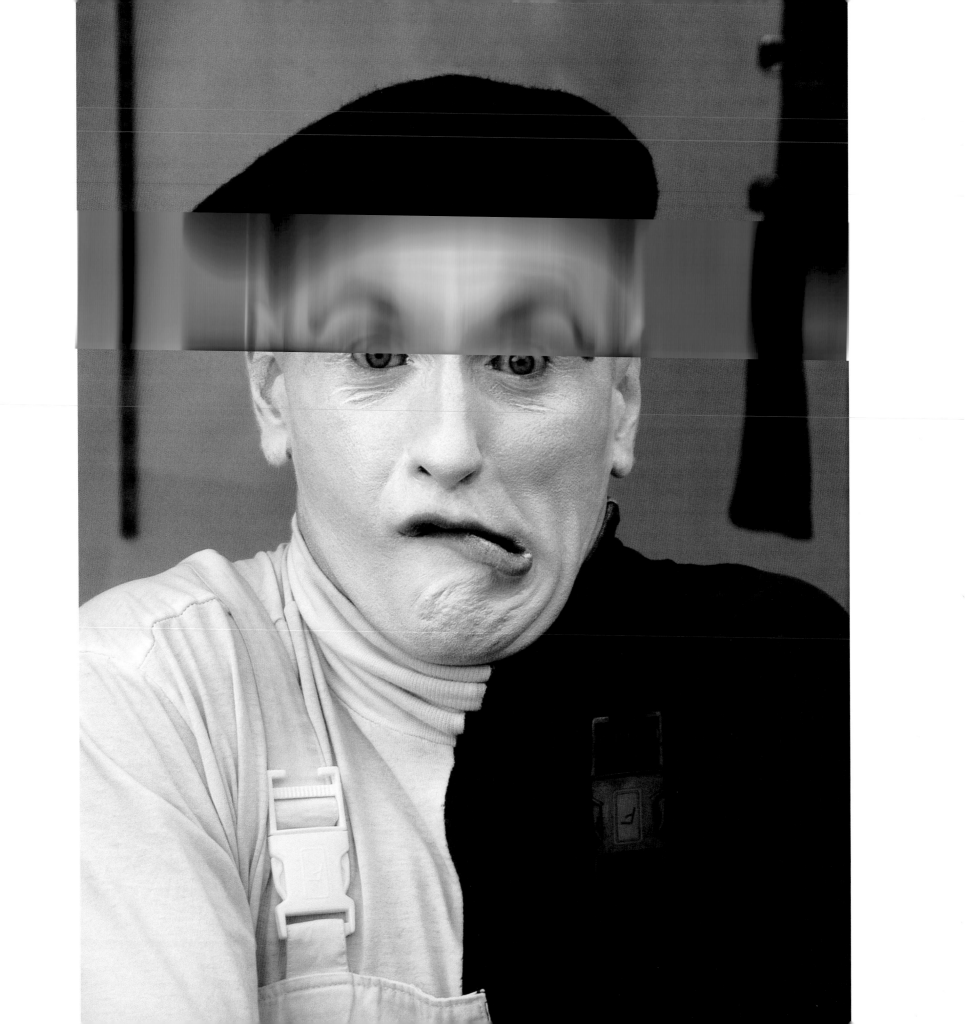

Udine

marble. The other side is dominated by the Renaissance-style Porticato di San Giovanni with white marble arches (left).

Piazza Matteotti, the town's other large square, is surrounded by arcades with fashionable shops and lively cafés. In centuries past this *piazza* was known as "justice square" because of the many executions that took place there. Today it is a busy meeting place and a popular gathering spot. Children play in Piazza Matteotti (below), climbing on the fountain in the middle of the square while parents sit in nearby cafés supervising and socializing.

UDINE IS FILLED WITH MAGNIFICENT ARCHITECTURE. *The Venetian influence on Loggia del Lionello is obvious. Streetlights reflect on its polished pink and white marble (top left). Mosaics (bottom left) in an adjacent bar shimmer*

in the light. Late at night Piazza Matteotti shines with a warm, golden glow (above). The Church of San Giacomo,
one of the oldest churches in Udine, was built in 1378 and the baroque façade was added during the 16ᵗʰ century.

PIAZZA MATTEOTTI is surrounded by arcades with many fashionable boutiques, outdoor cafés, and bars underneath them. The women of Udine typically are stylish, fit, and attractive (left). Because Udine is relatively flat, many townspeople ride bikes to shop and do errands (right).

Cortina d'Ampezzo

Set in a lush mountain valley guarded by stunning peaks, Cortina d'Ampezzo (right) is Italy's most exclusive ski resort and summer retreat. Chiseled limestone spires and jagged mountains surround the town and turn golden when lit by the sun. The town is surrounded by the dramatic scenery of the Dolomiti d'Ampezzo Natural Park. Through strict zoning, the people of the Ampezzo Valley have preserved the area's natural beauty and Tyrolean architecture, making it one of the most beautiful resorts in the country.

During the summer, Cortina is in full bloom and a feast for the eyes. Dazzling window boxes and planters (below), crammed full with colorful flowers, are on display everywhere. The town is a popular destination for Italians from Venice and Milan who come to enjoy the fresh mountain air. On weekends the town is filled with fashionable people hoping to escape the rigors of city life. Cortina is a place to see and be seen and has always drawn the wealthy and powerful to its streets and slopes. Weekend evenings Piazza Venezia and the Corso Italia are crowded with well-dressed Italians. This pedestrian thoroughfare, lined with many luxury shops, is a window-shopper's paradise.

LIFE ALONG CORSO ITALIA, Cortina's popular pedestrian street, is busy. A mother and daughter (left), dressed in Tyrolean inspired clothes, rush down the sidewalk and a young woman (above) brings coffee to her companions.

Following pages:

THE ELEGANT HOTEL ANCORA, situated on Piazza Venezia, is located in the heart of Cortina. In the summer its wooden Tyrolean decks are filled with flowers. Three dogs stand amid the flowers, intently observing the activities in the piazza below.

IN CORTINA, PEOPLE FREQUENTLY DRESS in Tyrolean clothing. Two attractive women walk to a special event in formal attire (left). A young woman, along with her daughter and the family dog (above), stops in front of Bulgari to ogle the jewelry display.

THE NORTH FACE COMPANY set up a climbing wall in Cortina's piazza. In the evening, guides harnessed kids and let them climb to the top with a guide rope. A rapt crowd gathers at the bottom of the wall and watches (lower) as a boy repels down (right).

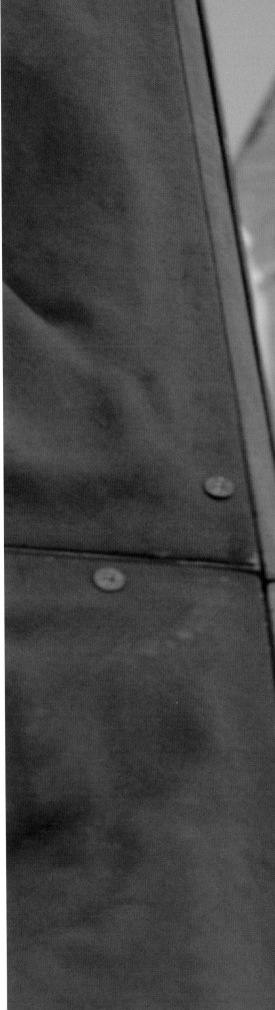

Orta San Giulio

The stunning town of Orta San Giulio and its Piazza Principale sit peacefully on the shores of Lake Orta in the foothills of the Alps. From the square there is a glorious view of Isola San Giulio with its historic 12th century basilica (right). Speedboats zip to and from the *piazza* all day long, taking tourists and weekend visitors to the island for a look around or a meal at an excellent lakeside restaurant. The speedboat captains like to relax in Piazza Principale, joking with each other and their customers while they wait for the next fare to Isola San Giulio. The *piazza* is delightful and has several lively restaurants and a popular wine bar. Children use the square as a playground while locals and visitors sit on tree-shaded benches, enjoying the views and the gentle breezes. At dusk the light in the *piazza* is spectacular and people watch the rays of the sun reflect upon the water (below).

DURING THE DAY TOURISTS AND WEEKEND VISITORS RENT BOATS *and enjoy rowing on the
lake. Outdoor cafés provide delicious food and gorgeous views of the lake (above). At dusk, a family walks
alongside the lake (right), bathed in the magical light of the setting sun.*

Aosta

Located near Mont Blanc, the highest mountain in the Alps, Aosta is [illegible] is Aosta's central square and charming pedestrian streets lead into it. The stunning Hôtel de Ville (town hall) is the largest and most impressive building on the square. During August the *piazza* hosts an exhibit for the area's talented regional artists. At night local artisans demonstrate their crafts, drawing many fascinated viewers. Aosta is home to a number of people who have relocated from Calabria, a region in southern Italy. The Calabrese, as they are called, continue to hold their folk festivals in Aosta during which they dress in traditional clothing (left and below).

PIAZZA EMILIO CHANOUX is the heart of Aosta and Café De La Place (right), its most popular meeting spot, is the pulse. On a quiet Sunday afternoon the piazza suddenly comes to life with the roar of motorcycles (top left). Later, a mother and daughter share an intimate moment in the square (bottom left).

CAFE' DE LA PLACE

AOSTA SITS IN A LUSH VALLEY at the confluence of two rivers. The hills surrounding the town loom just outside Aosta's ancient Roman arch (left). Between Aosta and the nearby French border horses graze beneath a massive glacier (right).

DURING THE SUMMER MONTHS, glaciers are visible from nearly every spot in town (right). In August the town of Aosta hosts an art exhibit to display local crafts, including intricate woodwork and carvings (below). Each night in the piazza the artisans demonstrate their skills.

LIGURIA

Camogli

Camogli translates as "house of wives." It was so named because in centuries past, when their husbands were out to sea, the women ran the town. Camogli is blessed with two unique *piazze*. Piazza Colombo hugs the harbor where the fishing fleet is moored and nets often hang nearby to dry. In August local fishermen and Italians on holiday share this quaint village. Fishermen with faces weathered by sun and wind usually sit around the edge of the *piazza*. They mend nets and hold court while gorgeous, bikini-clad young women stroll by (below).

A short walk through a nearby tunnel reveals another small *piazza* that kisses the beach and provides magical views of the shimmering Ligurian coastline. Colorful buildings with *trompe-l'oeil* paintings offer visitors a glimpse of an elegant era gone by. Children of all ages play together along the beach (right) and in the adjacent square. It seems as though everyone in Camogli is happy in this beautiful paradise by the sea.

ITALIANS FROM ALL OVER THE COUNTRY *flock to Camogli to frolic on its shores and escape the summer heat. Young girls discuss important matters in the square that overlooks the beach (left) while another takes aim at a playmate with her squirt gun (above).*

CAMOGLI, ORIGINALLY A BUSY FISHING PORT, *is also now a summer retreat. The bows of two colorful fishing boats bob gently in the harbor (below). Red beach chairs along the water's edge wait patiently for beachgoers in Santa Margherita, a four-minute train ride from Camogli (right).*

*ITALIAN TOURISTS are silhouetted
as they try a hand at fishing (right).
A fisherman mends his nets (top left)
while another shows off his catch of the
day—a small octopus (above).*

ACTIVITIES FOR YOUNGSTERS *take place in the town center throughout the day. The sparkling waves and rocky green hills provide a beautiful backdrop for teenagers during an impromptu game of volleyball in the square.*

LIGURIA

Cinque Terre

Visiting the Cinque Terre (Five Lands) is like taking a trip back in time. Five quaint and colorful fishing villages along the sea are strung together by an ancient walking path. Each village has a distinct personality. In Riomaggiore boats fill the harbor near the *piazza* and local men gather there to talk about the day's catch, discuss politics, or tell tall tales. Manarola's *piazza* overlooks a swimming cove where local boys take turns diving from rocks high above the sea. Corniglia is perched high above the Ligurian Sea and is the most difficult village to reach because of a steep climb up many steps. Vernazza is the most picturesque of the five towns and its small, intimate *piazza* hugs the sea (right). Monterosso al Mare, the largest of the five, has several *piazze* and the most popular one includes a playground where children swing, climb, slide, and play soccer. All of the towns rely heavily on the sea and the land, as fishing and farming on the steep hillsides have sustained the area's inhabitants throughout many centuries.

Young lovers rest near the Via dell'Amore footpath (above).

MEN SIT AMID BOATS in a tiny, makeshift piazza, telling stories
about "the one that got away"(right). This man (above) has been farming the
steep hillsides above the town of Monterosso al Mare for decades.

ON A HOT SUMMER AFTERNOON MUSICIANS (above) entertain tourists on the promenade
along the Ligurian shore. A group (right) gathers for a late afternoon drink at an outdoor café in a small,
intimate piazza tucked away in a corner of Monterosso al Mare.

Sciacchetrà
5 Terre d.o.c
Grappa 5 Terre
Arancino di Monterosso
Limoncino delle 5 Terre
Elisir d'Erbe del
Parco delle 5 Terre
Acciughe Salate
Pesto e Salse
Liguri

A DOG SLEEPILY WATCHES THE WORLD GO BY outside a café while his owner stops for a drink *(below). A young woman wearing a red sweater walks with her loyal companion (right), passing a woman knitting in the piazza. Could she be knitting another red sweater?*

FLORENCE

Piazza della Signoria

The famous Café Rivoire in Florence's beautiful Piazza della Signoria offers its clientele a prime spot for viewing the square's exquisite sculptures, along with some of the best people-watching in all of Italy. Spending time in this *piazza* means observing a wide variety of characters and events throughout the day. Local residents scurry through the square on an errand or a break from work. Tourists admire the majestic statues as horse-drawn carriages wait patiently for a new fare. The ubiquitous well-groomed Carabinieri stand guard, and tour groups gawk at Palazzo Vecchio as guides talk animatedly. On warm summer days and evenings, the busy outdoor cafés and restaurants that surround the square fill with tourists and Italians alike.

The *palazzo* is an excellent example of medieval architecture and reveals the mighty power and wealth of the Florentine Republic in centuries past.

Much of Florence's history has been played out in the square, including Savonarola's Bonfire of the Vanities and his subsequent execution.

The Arno River (right) flows through the heart of Florence. It divides the city in half and is a popular spot for rowing teams to practice their sport. The Ponte Vecchio, a Florentine landmark, is a pedestrian bridge that links the two sides of the city. Once filled with butcher stalls, it is now lined with upscale jewelry shops.

Elegant architecture provides a stunning reflection in a window near the square (left).

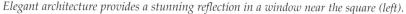

PIAZZA DELLA SIGNORIA IS ALWAYS HOPPING WITH ACTIVITY. A young girl and a horse (above) slowly get acquainted as he awaits his next fare. Café Rivoire (right), at the west end of the square, is the perfect spot to order a refreshing drink and watch people.

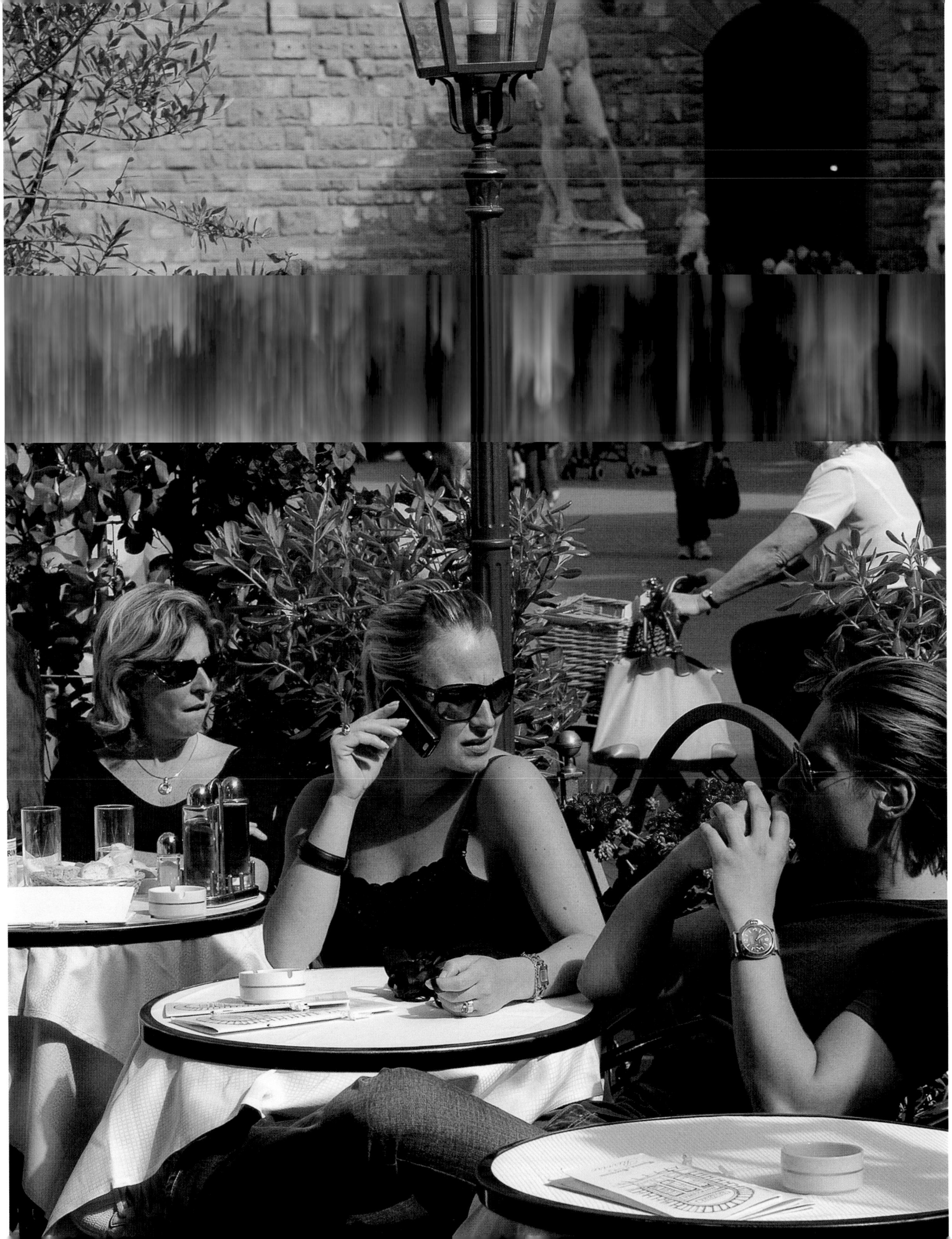

PIAZZA DELLA SIGNORIA *is
simply stunning at night.
The imposing Palazzo Vecchio,
with its giant bell tower, was
built in 1322 and still serves
as Florence's town hall.
The Loggia dei Lanzi (on the
right), built 60 years later,
showcases sculpture from the
16th century.*

HANDSOME AND INTERESTING PEOPLE *frequent this piazza.*
On a warm, summer afternoon a dapper gentleman (left) strolls among the crowds and
a beautiful young woman (above), bathed in golden light, gazes out across the square.

FLORENCE

Piazza di Santa Croce

Every June during the Festival of San Giovanni, the patron saint of the city of Florence, the beautiful Piazza di Santa Croce (right) is transformed into a sandy field for the annual Calcio Storico, a wild football tournament that originated in the 16th century. Teams representing each of the four quarters of Florence play in two separate games and the winners meet in a playoff match. This medieval contest is preceded by a dazzling procession of residents dressed in colorful costumes who parade around the square.

The free-for-all football game follows the parade. Players, also dressed in period costumes, do not have the protective benefit of pads or helmets. By the end of the chaotic match, which appears to be a combination of rugby, football, and wrestling, most of the players' shirts have been torn off and some players even walk away bloody. As was customary during the Renaissance, the winning team is awarded a white cow (below).

VIVIDLY COLORED COSTUMES *are a big part of the tradition of Calcio Storico. An intense player (above),*

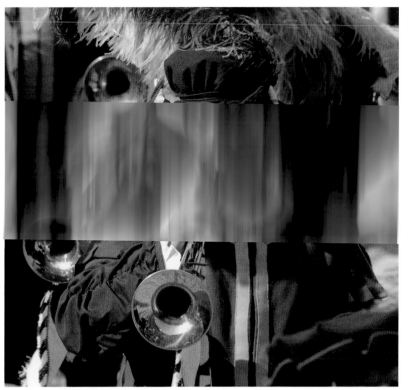

encrusted with mud, walks past the medieval flag bearers. The trumpet and drum corps entertain the crowd before the start of the game (above).

PASSION RUNS *at a fever pitch during the match, both on the field and in the stands. The game is rough, and players tackle potential defenders, pinning them to the ground.*

THE GAME OFTEN DESCENDS INTO CHAOS; *few rules are apparent. At the end of the match players are hot, sweaty, and completely drained (above). The crowd watches as a brawl erupts in the corner of the piazza after a score (right).*

TUSCANY

Lucca

Lucca, a charming walled city, sits below the Apennines in northwestern Tuscany. Originally settled by Etruscans, it later became a thriving Roman colony. The geographic heart of the city is Piazza San Michele in Foro where residents have gathered for more than two millennia. During the Roman Empire the *piazza* was the original site of the forum, and today it is one of the most popular meeting places in Lucca. The largest building on the square is a magnificent Romanesque church.

One block away in Piazza Napoleone, the largest square in Lucca, we saw young *sbandieratori* (flag-wavers) performing for a large crowd (right). As we photographed them, they asked many questions about the United States. The most pressing question was: "Is the Statue of Liberty taller than our medieval tower in Lucca?"

Since the streets in town are flat and extremely narrow, most Lucchesi ride bikes. It is not uncommon to see vegetables, pizza, and other goods delivered by bicycle. Businessmen and women bike to work in stylish attire. One day we saw a well-dressed, elderly couple holding hands as they pedaled side by side through the *piazza*.

A BEAUTIFUL BRIDE (left) in an exotic designer gown waits outside the church in Piazza San Michele in Foro. The façade of the magnificent church reflects on the hood of the getaway car.

LUCCA IS THE BIRTHPLACE of the Italian composer Giacomo Puccini. Turandot Café (right), a popular gathering spot, is named for one of his operas. A dapper man on his bicycle (above) stops to check out the scene in the café.

IN PIAZZA NAPOLEONE
a young sbandieratori eyes
the flag he has thrown in the
air (left). He misses the
catch and the flag lands on
his head. A senior member
of the group checks to ensure
that he is not seriously

Val d'Orcia

Situated between Montepulciano and Montalcino, home of the

Piazza della Libertà in San Quirico d'Orcia is wonderfully enchanting; locals of all ages enjoy it throughout the day. Bar Centrale, the most popular spot, is where men play cards and children and parents enjoy *gelato*. Adjacent to the *piazza* is a scenic manicured park dating to the 16th century.

Piazza il Vecchietta in Castiglione d'Orcia, just a few miles down the road, is a tiny, exquisite square surrounded by medieval brick homes. At its center is an old well which at one time was the village's central meeting place but has since gone dry. Overlooking the *piazza* is "Rocca d'Orcia," an imposing medieval fortress.

The region is known for fine pecorino cheese (above). Sunflowers are abundant in the countryside (left).

THE LIVELIEST GATHERING SPOT in San Quirico d'Orcia is Bar Centrale (above). It is busy all day and well into the night. Men play cards (right) in front of a glass door that reflects the café's gelato stand. A friendly store clerk (far right), bathed in late afternoon light, waves to an acquaintance as she walks across the square towards the café.

PIAZZA IL VECCHIETTA in Castiglione d'Orcia is a quiet little square (right). There are a few homes, a small municipal building, and a tourist office in the piazza. Missing are the cafés, restaurants, and shops. The people who live around this little piazza are very friendly (above) and enjoy chatting with the occasional tourists who wander by.

126

IN SAN QUIRICO D'ORCIA A GROUP OF FRIENDLY MEN *sits in front of Bar Centrale,
surrounded by red flowers, talking about life (above). Cypress trees are emblematic of Tuscany.
These trees and a cross overlook a farmer's field close to town (right).*

TUSCANY

Arezzo

The antique fair centered in Piazza Grande in Arezzo, a charming Tuscan hill town, is a sight to behold. "Fiera Antiquaria," as it is called in Italian, is the country's largest and oldest antique marketplace. On the first weekend of every month, dealers and merchants come from all over Italy to display their collections. Rusted hardware, elegantly polished furniture, and small treasures (below) are displayed in booths in the main *piazza* and along nearby streets in the historical part of town.

Eccentric vendors and the market's bustling activity combine to create a festive atmosphere in the square. Sophisticated shoppers wander among booths in the *piazza* and along the steep streets looking for special objects to purchase. The wide array of antiques and collectibles offered at the fair is beyond imagination.

Tuscan specialty foods entice shoppers inside where the aromas are irresistible (right).

130

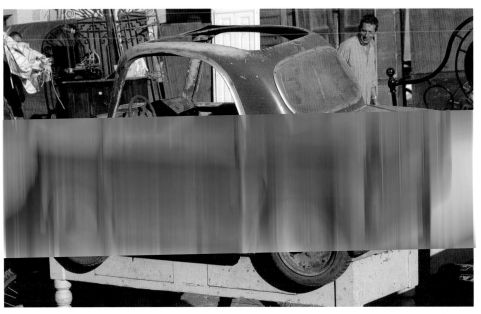

PIAZZA GRANDE IS FILLED with all sorts of antiques and collectibles during the monthly market (left). A dilapidated child's car (top right) waits for a new owner. A market vendor takes time out to read the newspaper amid his treasures (above).

PEOPLE DRESSED IN COSTUMES
from the Middle Ages mingle with
stylish shoppers on a narrow street lined
with antiques. Earlier in the day a
medieval parade had taken place in the
heart of the city.

Following pages:

COLORFUL GOBLETS SPARKLE
in an open-air stall at the antique market.
The glasses cast dazzling reflections in
the sunlight and shadows from one
glass fall upon another.

THE BUILDINGS ON THE NORTH SIDE OF THE PIAZZA are part of an outdoor arcade designed by Giorgio Vasari in the 16th century. A special candle-lit birthday celebration (left) is held under the beautiful arches. An attractive woman (above) takes a break from antique shopping.

Siena

Siena is situated on a site that was originally settled by the Etru~~...~~

~~...~~

~~...~~ 1348, killing two-thirds of its population. Eventually, after years of fighting with Florence, Siena was forced to surrender and came under the rule of its long-time archrival.

The central square, Piazza del Campo (left), was built on a field in 1349 and has been the heart of the city ever since. The *piazza* is shaped like an oyster shell. One side is devoted to municipal buildings, including the Gothic Torre del Mangia, which towers 328 feet above the square and provides breathtaking views of the Tuscan countryside. The opposite side of the square is filled with bustling outdoor cafés and restaurants.

A flag-waver (above), wearing the colors of his contrada, marches in the medieval pageant before the horse race.

The city of Siena is divided into 17 *contrade*, or neighborhoods. A citizen is in a particular *contrada* based on birthplace. It is where a person attends church, socializes, and learns about important life values. Each *contrada* has its own mascot such as a snail, giraffe, eagle, or unicorn.

It is almost impossible to describe the passion and enthusiasm that the Sienese

and August 16, religious feast days created in her honor.

During the week of the Palio, members of the *contrade* wear scarves with their respective colors and mascots. Only ten horses can run in the Palio, and a lottery is held to determine which *contrade* will race. Selected contestants then draw a horse and jockey in a subsequent lottery. On the day of the Palio, each *contrada's* horse is taken into the neighborhood church and blessed by

the priest. The only rule of the extremely competitive race is that jockeys may not interfere with another horse's reins. Even a rider-less horse can be crowned a winner. Chicanery is common, even to the point of kidnapping another *contrada's* horse or jockey. The pageantry surrounding the Palio is majestic and colorful. Festivities include a grand procession through town and the *piazza* by residents outfitted in an array of sumptuous, medieval costumes.

FROM THE MOMENT THE HORSE IS SELECTED in the lottery, the barberesco (contrada's groom) does not leave the horse's side until after the Palio (left). The night before the race tables line the streets of the neighborhood for the contrada dinner (above), where members of the contrada enhearten their jockey.

AFTER A HISTORICAL PROCESSION in Renaissance-inspired costumes, the Carabinieri Cavalry mesmerizes the Palio crowd. Just before the official race begins, they charge on horseback around Piazza del Campo at a full gallop with swords drawn and hooves pounding.

144

FLAGS OF THE CONTRADE, *chosen by lottery for the upcoming Palio, flutter on the outside of a building (left). Costumes for the grand procession that precedes the race are well-researched and are the result of a collaboration between historians, costume designers, and tailors. A handsome young man (above) marches through the square, elaborately dressed as a warrior.*

147

AS HAS BEEN THE CUSTOM for centuries, the starting gate
is a simple rope. Drawing lots determines the order in which the horses line
up. The riders are aggressive and very focused at the start of the race (left).
To be Sienese is to be passionate about the Palio, starting at a young age.
Girls from the Unicorn Contrada cheer wildly (above) for their
horse during a trial race.

Gubbio

UMBRIA

The town of Gubbio is perched on the lower slopes of

[text obscured/illegible] Middle Ages. Our friend Emilia, who lives in Gubbio, says that the Eugubini (Gubbio residents) enjoy being considered crazy. They are certainly crazed with emotion during the Corsa dei Ceri.

The Corsa dei Ceri (left) takes place each year on May 15th, the eve of the anniversary of the death of the town's patron saint, Ubaldo Baldassini. The festival has been celebrated without interruption since the 12th century. Its exact origins are unknown, but many scholars believe that it is based on old pagan beliefs involving Ceres, the Roman goddess of plants and meadows.

Worshippers bless themselves on the street outside of mass in the stonemasons' church (above).

The event is so important to the people of Gubbio that during World War II, when all the young men from the town were away fighting, the women upheld the tradition of racing the *ceri* through town and up the steep path to Basilica di Sant'Ubaldo, which is perched atop Monte Ingino.

The three *ceri*, made of heavy wood,

. . . . of the day begin when drummers dressed in medieval costumes march through town at dawn to awaken the *ceraioli* (the *ceri* bearers). A special mass is held in the small church belonging to the stonemasons' guild. At midday, the townspeople, who dress in yellow, black, and blue shirts signifying their respective guilds, are heralded to the square to observe the raising of the *ceri* amid officials and musicians dressed in medieval costumes. As the *ceraioli* circle the *piazza* three times, the crowd cheers wildly.

In the late afternoon the *ceri* are brought back into Piazza Grande and the crowd erupts again, yelling feverishly and waving their hands. The passion and fervor of the group is unparalleled. As the *ceri* leave the square for the race to the top of the mountain, throngs of people scream: "*Vai! Vai! Vai!*" (Go! Go! Go!) The young men who bear the *ceri* then dash through town and run up the steep 1,000-foot incline to the top of Monte Ingino. Saint Ubaldo's guild always leads the way to the basilica where all *ceraioli* receive a special blessing.

AT A VERY EARLY AGE kids wear the costume of their group (right). Wearing the colors of their guild, young boys practice with a small version of a cero (left). Every year a children's ceri race is held the week following the ceri festival.

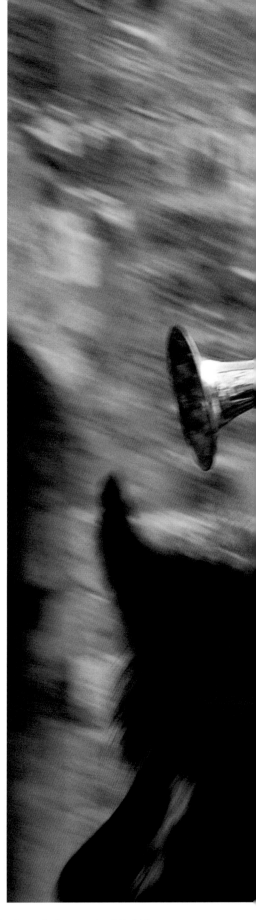

BEFORE THE RACE a bishop, other clergy, policemen, and Carabinieri (above) lead the procession of a statue of Saint Ubaldo through the streets of Gubbio.

A TRUMPETER IN MEDIEVAL DRESS (above) rides through town announcing the ceri's return to Piazza Grande.

THE CERI ARE HOISTED UPRIGHT *in the jam-packed Piazza Grande before a wildly enthusiastic crowd (left). A statue of Saint George rides a horse on top of one cero, while Saint Anthony, in black, sits atop the other. A man from Saint Anthony's guild leans out of a window (above) to touch the statue with the hope that his prayers will be answered.*

Gubbio Crossbow

While the Corsa dei Ceri is certainly the most exciting

... by Gubbio's world-famous
sbandieratori (flag-wavers, left) who dress in colorful costumes
from the Middle Ages. Several of the flags are representative
of ancient Umbrian, the language spoken by the original
inhabitants of the area who preceded the Romans.

Crossbow contestants (above) are silhouetted in front of the target against the ancient town hall.

161

THE CROSSBOW CONTEST is multi-generational. A father encourages his son and helps him line up the shot (above top). After the boy hits the target's center, the father gives him a proud hug (above bottom). Competitors from both towns show the target to the judges (right) who determine the winning team.

UMBRIA

Norcia

Snuggled in the mountainous region of eastern Umbria is the little town of Norcia. It is known as the "Butcher Shop of Rome" for such specialties as wild boar hams and sausages, prized black truffles, and tasty Castelluccio lentils. Piazza San Benedetto is the geometric and social center of this small town. The forum of the Roman colony of Nursia was near the square's current location. Eight streets radiate out to the corners of the town from the *piazza*. In the center stands a statue of St. Benedict who was born in Norcia during the 8th century and was the founder of the first monastic order. St. Benedict is the namesake of Pope Benedict XVI and is the patron saint of both Europe and Norcia.

Every July, during the feast day of St. Benedict,

residents celebrate the arrival of a torch from a different European city. In 2005 the torch arrived from Moscow. The celebration includes fireworks, a reception for visiting dignitaries, and religious services led by two local bishops and attended by visiting cardinals from Rome. Festivities continue the next afternoon when citizens dress in medieval costumes (left) and parade from the corners of the town, meeting in the center of the *piazza* at the statue of St. Benedict (right). This is followed by a crossbow tournament in full medieval costume as well as church services.

164

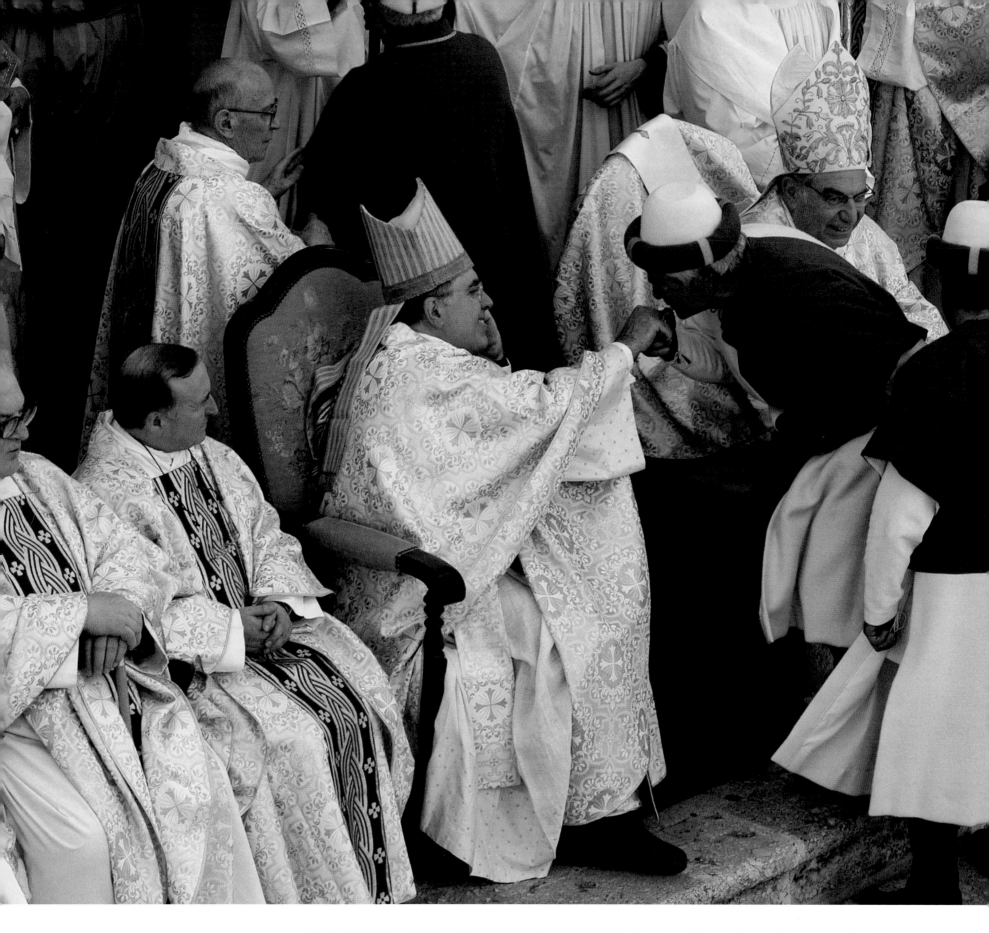

166   *TWO BISHOPS OBSERVE THE ELABORATE PAGEANT in the piazza. Afterwards, participants stream into the church for a religious celebration. As they enter they greet the bishops and kiss their rings—an age-old tradition (above).*

Three cardinals from Rome (top right), representing Pope Benedict XVI, attend the celebration. The head of Italy's Senate endures a media frenzy as he is interviewed (bottom right) on the steps of the municipal building.

IN THE COUNTRYSIDE AROUND NORCIA *wild boar roam and truffles abound. In Norcia and throughout Latium, butcher shops specializing in these delicacies are called "Norcineria." A butcher rearranges the display outside his shop in a small piazza (left). Two close friends walk through Piazza San Benedetto engrossed in conversation (below).*

CITIZENS OF NORCIA excitedly await the arrival of a torch from Moscow as dignitaries look on from the balcony of the town hall. A marching band keeps the crowd entertained during the wait.

SPEECHES BY SEVERAL DIGNITARIES *follow the arrival of the torch in the piazza.*
Also in attendance are officials from the Russian Orthodox Church. The celebration concludes with a
sensational display of fireworks in the square accompanied by Beethoven's glorious "Ode to Joy."
The piazza's statue of St. Benedict towers in the foreground (above and left).

Orvieto

Orvieto sits atop a volcanic hill overlooking lush vineyards. It lies

...water was actually transformed into the body of Christ. During his prayer, the communion wafer began to drip blood, turning the altar cloth a deep shade of red. When Pope Urban IV, who was visiting Orvieto at the time, heard of the miracle and confirmed it, he ordered that a magnificent cathedral be built in Orvieto to commemorate the event. He also established a religious holiday, Corpus Christi, in honor of the miracle. Now the cathedral draws people from all corners of the world and Piazza Duomo, where it is located, is always filled with visitors and locals (below) who admire the elaborate facade.

TWO PRIESTS PRESIDE OVER A FIRST COMMUNION CEREMONY in a dramatic chapel within the grand Duomo. The children, dressed in white robes with hoods (above), are dwarfed by the impressive scale of the room. Details of the cathedral's façade shimmer in the sunlight (right).

A YOUNG BOY CLAMBERS *upon his father's motor scooter parked in the piazza and pretends to drive (below). Orvieto's Romanesque-Gothic Duomo was begun in 1290, and was not completed until three centuries later. The gold façade and white marble towers of the cathedral catch the sun and are visible from a great distance away (right).*

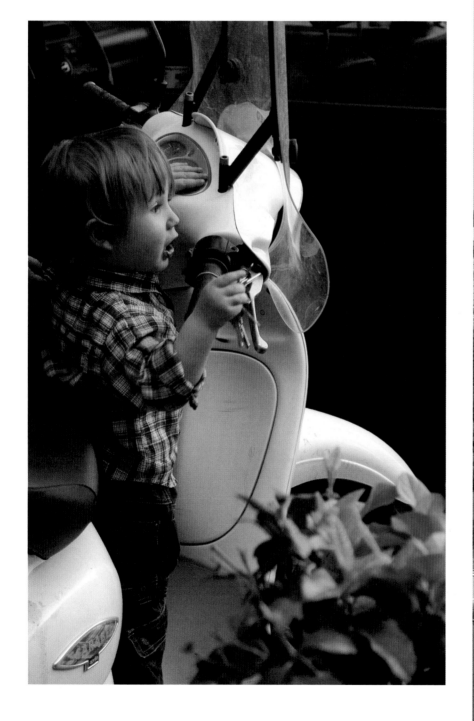

*THE CATHEDRAL AT NIGHT
(left) is bathed in soft orange, pearl,
and green light. An artist (right) sits
on the steps of the cathedral sketching
the piazza. A bas-relief depicting
stories from the Book of Genesis is
carved into the church facade*

Following pages:

*THE CATHEDRAL IS REFLECTED
in the windshield of a car. Details of
its famous rose window are visible,
including intricate niches with
surrounding sculptures. The large
gable above the window is a mosaic of
"The Coronation of the Virgin." The
mosaic on the left gable is "Mary's
Wedding" and on the right is "The
Presentation of Mary."*

Vatican City

When we arrived in Rome on April 14th, 2005, to begin work on our book, the city was in mourning for the beloved Pope John Paul II. We went straight to Vatican City and its majestic Piazza San Pietro. In spite of the heavy rain, long lines snaked along the entire length of the square as people filed slowly into St. Peter's Basilica to pay last respects to the Pope—it was a dreary scene.

Two days later the College of Cardinals began their conclave to elect the Pope's successor. The media swarmed the *piazza*. Visitors, priests, and nuns were ready for a long wait. The crowds talked quietly, prayed, and waited patiently. There was a great deal of confusion over the color of the smoke at the end of

each round of balloting. Everyone knew that black smoke coming from the chimney of the Sistine Chapel meant that no cardinal had received enough votes to become Pope. Alternately, white smoke signaled that there was indeed a new Pope. After the first day, the smoke appeared white but then turned black. In the late afternoon of the second day of voting, everyone watched as the dark smoke turned white but the bells did not toll (right). After about 15 minutes the bells finally began to ring. The entire *piazza* erupted in a palpable explosion of joy. People poured into the square from nearby apartments, hotels, and cafés. Everyone cheered and waved flags when the historic announcement was made: *"Habemus Papam!"* ("We have a Pope!" above).

A GROUP OF MEN IN BLUE ROBES watch the chimney of the Sistine Chapel intently, waiting for a sign that a new Pope has been chosen (above left). Nuns gather together (above right) in St. Peter's Square to pray during the long wait.

IMMEDIATELY AFTER THE BELLS *begin to toll, the piazza fills with people (following pages) anxious
to learn who has been elected. The wait seems interminable before Pope Benedict XVI steps out onto the balcony.
The crowd cheers when they learn that Cardinal Ratzinger has been chosen.*

A PRIEST clutches his prayer book and rosary as he awaits the news (right). When the bells ring, indicating that a new Pope has been chosen, the crowd erupts (left and above) with jubilation and people move hurriedly to the front of St. Peter's Basilica to listen to the new Pope address the crowd.

*ST. PETER'S BASILICA
is reflected in the calm waters
of the Tiber River in early
morning light. The Vatican is
an independent country
surrounded on all sides
by the city of Rome. It is the
world headquarters of the
Roman Catholic Church.*

Piazza di S. Maria in Trastevere

It has been said that if you want to glimpse what everyday life was like in ancient Rome, you should visit the Trastevere section of the city with its narrow, winding, cobblestone streets. Trastevere, which means "the other side of the Tiber River," was originally a working-class neighborhood and has recently become a desirable place to live. Wealthy Italians and expatriates live in the area and use Piazza di Santa Maria in Trastevere as a favorite gathering place.

Life bursts forth in this gem of a *piazza*. Tourists mingle with locals. Little boys practice riding bikes with training wheels, little girls push doll carriages, and people of all ages enjoy mouth-watering *gelato*. Children pick up an early passion for soccer under the watchful eyes of their parents. On Sunday mornings the cafés in the square fill rapidly with people reading newspapers; some read as many as three different papers in one sitting. Priests greet parishioners in the *loggia* of the church and carry on animated conversations. Multi-generational families gather after mass for a quick *cappuccino* and then head off to "*nonna's*" house for Sunday dinner.

A fountain near the center of the *piazza* is a magnet for people. Children like to climb on the base of it while parents lounge on the steps watching them. Amateur musicians often sit there and strum guitars, hoping that passersby will drop a coin or two into their cases. Tourists rest on the steps and read guidebooks while they study the intricate mosaics on the façade of the church.

The church of Santa Maria in Trastevere is the dominant building in the *piazza*. It is believed to be on the site of the oldest Christian church in Rome. The original church was built during the 4th century and was the very first church dedicated to the Virgin Mary. The current church, its apse beautifully decorated with shimmering mosaics (right), dates from the 12th century.

Nightlife thrives in the *piazza*. Young people enjoy socializing in the clubs and bars in this ancient section of the city. The restaurants overflow with customers during the evening hours and the intoxicating smells of garlic and tomato sauce waft into the square. Lively accordion music entertains all who sit in the square, whether they are in an outdoor café or relaxing on the fountain steps.

Candles, lit for special intentions, glimmer inside the church (above).

A MOSAIC OF "THE CORONATION OF THE VIRGIN" adorns the apse of Santa Maria in Trastevere.

198

A NEWLY MARRIED BRIDE AND GROOM KISS outside the church of Santa Maria in Trastevere as their friends and family shower them with rice.

A MAN RESTS ON THE STEPS leading to the fountain in the middle of the piazza while his parrot chatters and gestures animatedly (above). A well-groomed woman (right) rides her bicycle through the square, perhaps on her way to a party.

ON SUNDAY MORNINGS *locals sit amid a sea of newspapers at the cafés*
in the square. They stay for hours, reading and drinking cappuccini
while families walk through the piazza on the way to church.

Campo de' Fiori

Campo de' Fiori, which means "field of flowers," is a *piazza* in Rome with a dual personality. It is a thriving market by day and a popular gathering spot by night. During the cool morning hours the market is in full swing and offers a staggering selection of fruits, vegetables, spices, nuts, cheeses, fish, meats, and gorgeous flowers. Locals come to shop early in the day and tourists gather to view this renowned market. By late afternoon the stalls have been dismantled and people of all ages trickle into the square for a drink or dinner. Late at night the *piazza* is an important meeting place for young people who spill out of the local bars into the square. The entire area throbs with hearty laughter, the clinking of glasses, and lively music.

Campo de' Fiori is one of the few *piazze* in Italy that does not have a church or municipal edifice within it; however, it has held many important political rallies. The statue in the middle of the square (right) is of Giordano Bruno, a monk who was executed for heresy in 1600 for suggesting that the earth circled the sun.

A beautiful, sun-kissed woman watches the piazza come to life in the late afternoon (above).

IN THE EARLY EVENING HOURS, the piazza throbs with activity. Friends and neighbors greet each other and purchase last-minute items for dinner. A young woman pauses during her errands to chat on her cell phone (left).

Following pages:

THE COLORFUL BOUNTY of Campo de' Fiori's market is world-renowned. A beautiful woman tests a piece of fruit for ripeness as the market reflects in her sunglasses.

207

A STYLISH COUPLE *leaves a pizzeria in the radiance of the evening's soft light. Friends gather for drinks or dinner in the piazza at dusk, after the day's bustling market activity.*

Sutri

The small town of Sutri was originally settled by Etruscans before the founding of Rome. The medieval village was built high on a hill and its tall, imposing buildings and stone walls make it look like a fortress (above). Piazza del Comune in Sutri has it all—Italians of all ages laugh, gossip, and gesture madly as they keep an eye on children and grandchildren, flirt with one another, or share drinks at one of the square's three cafés. The town's inhabitants are extremely friendly, and there is quite a cast of eccentric characters who live and work there. Michael Rips, the author of *Pasquale's Nose*, a memoir about his time in Sutri, writes about the old men who frequent the *piazza*; they move methodically to different places in the square depending on the heat and the time of day.

During the day, townspeople gather around the fountain in the square to talk and laugh. In the late evening, when everyone is home for dinner, the *piazza* is empty and quietly aglow (right).

THERE IS ALWAYS A CLUSTER OF ECCENTRIC OLD MEN who gather in Piazza del Comune (above). They watch over the daily happenings in the square, observing everything and talking quietly. The men are good friends, practically inseparable, a close-knit group. The piazza is surrounded by a variety of shops and historic homes that date as far back as the 16ᵗʰ century. Shadows and warm light fall upon a balcony in an alley a few steps away from the square (right).

214

CHILDREN LOVE THE FOUNTAIN *in the square (above and right). It is a special spot, reserved just for them, where they play together, usually under the watchful eyes of parents or grandparents. The social structure in Sutri's piazza is very distinct and the daily rhythms of the small town vary only rarely. The same groups of people tend to meet in the same spots, like clockwork, each day.*

216

APULIA & SICILY

Locorotondo

Locorotondo, in the sun-drenched province of Apulia, is located on the heel of Italy's boot. It is Italy's largest producer of olive oil and wine and is an agricultural power-house. The town, with buildings made of white plaster, is set around the top of a large rock formation. Its name, loosely translated, means "around the hill." This region of Apulia is known for its *trulli*, white-washed spherical buildings made of stone without mortar. The exact origin of this unique style of architecture is unknown. One legend claims that they were built during the Middle Ages so they could easily be disassembled when the tax collector was in the area.

In late April the town stages a three-day celebration of the feast day of San Giorgio, the town's patron saint. Piazza Dante and Piazza Vittorio Emanuele (right), the main gathering spots, are decorated in beautiful lights. The festivities include religious celebrations and a procession (below), musical concerts, fireworks, and a competitive bicycle race.

PARTICIPANTS in Locorotondo's bike race are intense and extremely competitive. They follow a course that circles the town many times. Racers must ride up and down the hill that divides the town from the plains below. As they zip through the piazza (left),

MUSIC IS A BIG PART OF THE CELEBRATION *of the feast day of San Giorgio. All day and late into the night for three days, several different orchestras and bands alternate playing in one of two neighboring piazze.*

THIS TRULLI, VIEWED FROM THE MAIN PIAZZA IN LOCOROTONDO, is on a verdant plain situated below the centro storico (historical center) of the town.

Taormina

Taormina, suspended high above the sea on the slopes of Mount Tauro, is a lively town with spectacular views. The snowcapped peak of Mount Etna (right) and the volcanic smoke it emits are visible from the center of town. Taormina has long been a favorite springtime destination for northern Europeans due to its mild climate and sunny weather. The area was originally settled by early Greeks who left behind a beautiful amphitheater that Romans later used for gladiator contests. Today, during July and August, the space is home to "Taormina Arte," a festival of theater, dance, and music.

The town's two principle *piazze*, Piazza Duomo and Piazza IX Aprile, are linked by a busy pedestrian street lined with attractive shops. *Limoncello*, marzipan, and colorful Sicilian ceramics fill the windows and tempt passersby. Children frolic in the *piazze*, bringing toys (below), bikes, and miniature cars to the squares with them. Both *piazze* seem to float above the sea, buoyed by gentle breezes, where tourists and residents alike meet and mingle.

226

AN ENIGMATIC YOUNG WOMAN
walks into the piazza and offers a slow
smile as she looks directly at her
admirers (left). There are commanding
views from both of Taormina's piazze.
In Piazza IX Aprile a man and his best
friend (right) enjoy a soothing offshore
breeze as they look out at the calm
waters of the Ionian Sea.

*AN OLD MAN, BACKLIT BY THE EARLY MORNING SUN, works at remodeling
a small shop along Corso Umberto (above), the pedestrian street and primary
shopping avenue in Taormina. Street lamps glow in the piazza as people gather for
a reception in the square (right).*

228

MARZIPAN, DECORATIVE CANDIES made from ground almonds and egg whites, are popular throughout Sicily. The candies in Taormina are particularly beautiful and reflect a high degree of craftsmanship.

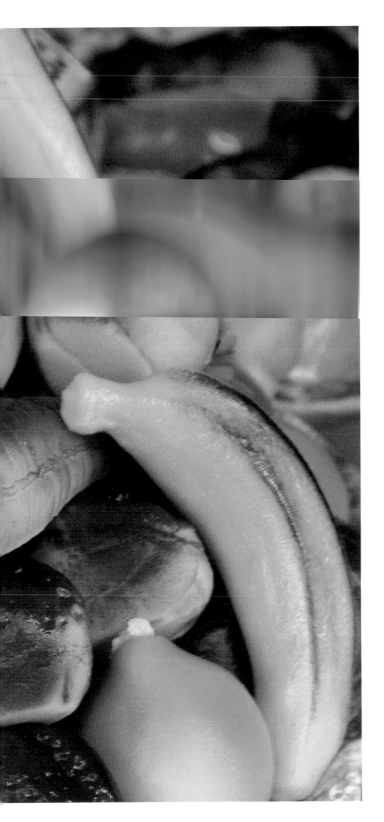

LEMON TREES abound throughout southern Italy and Sicily. Italians have been making an enchanting lemon drink called limoncello for centuries.

THIS IS A NEW TWIST ON AN OLD STORY. *Boy meets girl in the piazza.*
He entices her aboard his motorcycle (above). A few minutes later she commandeers
his bike and lets him have a ride (right).

Cefalù

Cefalù, "the pearl of the Mediterranean," is located on Sicily's northern shore and boasts a large, gorgeous beach. It is a favorite springtime vacation getaway for many Europeans where they can enjoy the warm weather and relaxed lifestyle. Piazza Duomo, anchored by the cathedral, is flanked by shops, several bustling cafés, and a municipal building, making the square the most lively area of the city. The majestic cathedral (right), begun in 1131, was commissioned by Roger II, after he made a bargain with God to build a church in His honor if God spared him during a fierce storm at sea.

The remains of a Greek temple to Diana, possibly dating from the 5th century BC, and the crumbling remnants of a fortress from the Middle Ages are perched on a rock precipice above the town. From there, the views of the red-tiled roofs of Cefalù and the Sicilian coastline (below) are spellbinding.

INSIDE CEFALÙ'S NORMAN CATHEDRAL *are some of Sicily's most impressive Byzantine mosaics.*
The ceiling displays a gigantic, glittering gold mosaic of Christ the Almighty who looks down upon his worshippers.
Outside, after a wedding ceremony, a bride and groom kiss (left) while a crowd looks on approvingly. The bride and her
glamorous girlfriends pose for a photographer in the church's courtyard, just up from Piazza del Duomo (above).

LUNGOMARE BEACH IS ILLUMINATED WITH GOLD LIGHT at sunset while people play along the shores of the Tyrrhenian Sea. The twin towers of the Norman cathedral dominate the town's skyline. Ancient ruins have been unearthed at Rocca di Cefalù, the large rock formation on the right. The beach and the sea's balmy waters are a magnet for tourists, many of whom return year after year to soak up Sicily's abundant sunshine.

— *Acknowledgements* —

After writing a book like this, there are so many people to thank, on both sides of the Atlantic. First, this book would still be in the daydream stage if it were not for Kendall Nelson. She believed in the project from the very beginning and encouraged us to pursue it. The beautiful design and layout would not have been possible without Constance H. Phelps, who started out as our teacher and has become our friend. Thank you to Connie and Kendall for truly believing in us.

We were lucky to have exceptional photography teachers who taught us with passion and precision: Marsha Reifman instructed us on how to use our cameras, Jim Stanfield instilled the concept that a photograph can always be improved, Eddie Soloway showed us how to really see, Arthur Meyerson opened our eyes about great color, David Julian tutored us patiently on the technical aspects of working with digital files, and Jay Maisel taught us about color, light, and gesture and encouraged us to give the book a try.

There are so many people in Italy who were incredibly kind and helpful to us; a few stand out

A HANDSOME GONDOLIER
glides his boat along Venice's
Grand Canal with the church of
Santa Maria della Salute
in the background.

as having gone above and beyond. Federico Bianconi in Norcia helped us in countless ways and the entire Bianconi family redefined the term "hospitality." The town of Norcia welcomed us with open arms for which we are very thankful. Emilia Valentini has become a new friend and provided us with fascinating information about Gubbio. Carlo Papini Giuriati, a long-time friend and the best guide in Rome, always provided us with whatever we needed, and Marco Achilli showered us with his generosity and friendship. We are thankful that Massimo Romagnoli suggested we visit Castiglione d'Orcia; his recommendation led us to discover the entire Val d'Orcia. There were other Italians who helped us along the way as well—the Piersanti family, Paola and Antonio Gugliotta, Fede Germani Rossi, and Alex Rossi.

Several friends suggested *piazze* for us to visit. Thank you to Susan Connelly for telling us about Sutri, Michael Verlander for encouraging us to visit Orta San Giulio, and Roger DeBard for suggesting Bevagna.

While producing this book we had excellent technical help. Ray Reed and Jim Armstrong at Tri-Digital Group did an amazing job with the pre-press, Janie Moran and the tireless team at F-Stop assisted with the processing, and the entire printing group at Worzalla was extremely helpful, especially Kitty Grigsby and Bonnie Kusmider.

Several people gave us invaluable advice, including our friend Dan Drackett, who helped with the book cover text and image selection, and Chuck Tampio, who refined our working title. Janet and Michael Verlander offered their expertise all along the way, from the conceptual through the marketing stages.

Our diligent editor, Carrie Lightner, was always helpful and efficient. Heartfelt thanks as well to our proofreaders—Susan Jackson, Katherine Melville, Anne Kalik, and Karen Vance.

Thank you most of all to the beautiful country of Italy and its wonderful people.